FAVORITE BRAND NAME

KRAFT
Diabetic
Choices

Publications International, Ltd.

Favorite Brand Name Recipes at www.fbnr.com

Introduction

Welcome to *Diabetic Choices*—an exciting new cookbook brought to you by the Kraft family of brands. Thanks to the easy and delicious recipes in this book, you and your whole family can enjoy healthful meals together.

Have a Plan

Be the best you can be now and in the future by creating an action plan to control your diabetes. Meet with a registered dietitian or a certified diabetes educator to develop a meal plan and exercise routine that is right for you. A good strategy will allow you to enjoy food and lead a fulfilling life.

Stay Active

Regular exercise can help improve body weight and blood glucose and may lower blood cholesterol levels. Exercise may also reduce your risk of high blood pressure and heart disease. Health experts advise adults to get 30 minutes of exercise daily.

You Have Choices

Fortunately, restrictive diets are a thing of the past. This doesn't mean you can eat anything you want whenever you want, but with an understanding of food exchange lists and carbohydrate counting, your meal choices are plentiful. Eating a balanced diet with a variety of foods in moderate amounts makes sense for everyone—not just for people living with diabetes.

Help Yourself

Learn as much as you can about diabetes. The more you know, the better you will feel. A positive attitude plus support from family and friends can go a long way.

Recipe Nutrition Know-How

Recipes in this book were developed according to nutrition recommendations set forth by the American Diabetes Association. Each recipe lists nutrition information per serving for calories, fat, carbohydrate and protein. Many recipes contain good-for-you nutrients, like fiber, vitamin A, vitamin C, calcium and iron. Exchange values are also given so you can see how a recipe can fit into your eating plan.

Some recipes are highlighted with special symbols, indicating they are low in fat or calories or good sources of fiber or calcium.

 Low Fat: contains 3 grams or less of fat per reference amount*

 Contains Fiber: contains 2½ grams or more of fiber per reference amount

 Good Source of Calcium: contains 10% or more of the daily value for calcium per reference amount

 Low Calorie: contains 40 calories or less per reference amount

Check Us Out!

Visit us at **www.kraftdiabeticchoices.com** to get more great recipes and nutrition information. You are just a click away from meal-planning tips, seasonal features, recipe contests and links to other websites about diabetes. Let us show you how easy it is to rely on Kraft for food products that turn your meal plan into delicious results your whole family will enjoy.

* Reference amount is specified by the government for food categories and is the basis for serving size.

Diabetic Choices

Lunch on the Run

Whether you're eating at home or on the go, you'll love this yummy assortment of great-tasting sandwiches.

Vegetable Turkey Pockets

Prep: 20 minutes plus refrigerating

¼ cup SEVEN SEAS FREE Ranch Fat Free Dressing
¼ cup KRAFT Mayo Light Mayonnaise
1 ½ cups LOUIS RICH Oven Roasted Turkey Breast strips
½ cup chopped cucumber
½ cup shredded carrot
1 small tomato, chopped
1 teaspoon dried basil leaves, crushed
2 pita breads, cut in half

MIX dressing, mayo, turkey, cucumber, carrot, tomato and basil. Refrigerate.

FILL pita bread halves with turkey mixture.

Makes 4 servings

Nutrition Information Per Serving: 200 calories, 6g total fat, 1g saturated fat, 20mg cholesterol, 870mg sodium, 27g carbohydrate, 2g dietary fiber, 10g protein

80% daily value vitamin A, 10% daily value vitamin C

Exchange: 1 Starch, 1 Carbohydrate, 1 Meat (L)

My Hero

Prep: 10 minutes

½ cup KRAFT Mayo Fat Free Mayonnaise Dressing
¼ cup KRAFT FREE Italian Fat Free Dressing
3 cups shredded lettuce
1 loaf (about 1 pound) French bread, split in half lengthwise
1 package (8 ounces) OSCAR MAYER FREE Fat Free Bologna
1 package (6 ounces) OSCAR MAYER FREE DELI-THIN Oven Roasted Fat Free Turkey Breast
2 medium tomatoes, thinly sliced
6 KRAFT FREE Singles Nonfat Process Cheese Product
1 medium green pepper, thinly sliced

MIX dressings.

TOSS lettuce with ¼ cup of the dressing mixture; set aside.

BRUSH cut surfaces of bread with remaining dressing mixture. Top bottom half of bread with lettuce mixture, meat, tomatoes, process cheese product and green pepper; cover with top half of bread. Cut sandwich into 8 pieces to serve.

Makes 8 servings

Nutrition Information Per Serving: 250 calories, 3g total fat, 0.5g saturated fat, 20mg cholesterol, 1320mg sodium, 40g carbohydrate, 3g dietary fiber, 16g protein

10% daily value vitamin A, 30% daily value vitamin C, 15% daily value calcium

Exchange: 2½ Starch, 1 Meat (VL)

My Hero

Diabetic Choices

Salads for Supper

Make your suppers super with this snazzy selection of main-dish salads.

Black Bean and Mango Chicken Salad

Prep: 10 minutes plus refrigerating

1 can (16 ounces) black beans, drained, rinsed
1 package (10 ounces) frozen corn, thawed
1 cup chopped ripe mango
½ pound boneless skinless chicken breasts, grilled, cut up
½ cup chopped red pepper
⅓ cup chopped fresh cilantro
⅓ cup chopped red onion
¼ cup lime juice
1 envelope GOOD SEASONS Italian Salad Dressing Mix

TOSS all ingredients in large bowl. Refrigerate.

SERVE with baked tortilla chips, if desired.

Makes 4 servings

Nutrition Information Per Serving: 250 calories, 2.5g total fat, 0.5g saturated fat, 35mg cholesterol, 990mg sodium, 40g carbohydrate, 7g dietary fiber, 20g protein

60% daily value vitamin A, 100% daily value vitamin C

Exchange: 2½ Carbohydrate, 1½ Meat (VL)

Grilled Steak Salad

Prep: 15 minutes   **Grill:** 14 minutes

¾ pound beef sirloin steak, ½ to ¾ inch thick
 1 teaspoon cracked pepper
10 cups torn romaine lettuce *or* 1 package (10 ounces)
    mixed salad greens
 1 beefsteak or other large tomato, cut into wedges
 1 small zucchini, sliced
½ cup slivered red onion
½ cup KRAFT LIGHT DONE RIGHT Thousand Island
    Reduced Fat Dressing

PLACE steak on grill over medium-hot coals. Sprinkle with pepper. Grill 5 to 7 minutes on each side to medium doneness.

CUT steak across grain into thin slices. Arrange all ingredients except dressing on individual plates. Serve with dressing.

Makes 4 servings

Tip: This recipe is a perfect way to use leftover cooked steak or roast beef.

Nutrition Information Per Serving: 230 calories, 9g total fat, 2.5g saturated fat, 55mg cholesterol, 370mg sodium, 15g carbohydrate, 4g dietary fiber, 22g protein

80% daily value vitamin A, 80% daily value vitamin C

Exchange: 3 Vegetable, 2 Meat (L), 1 Fat

Grilled Steak Salad

Grilled Chicken Caesar Salad

Prep: 15 minutes plus marinating   Grill: 20 minutes

    8 cups torn romaine lettuce
    1 pound boneless skinless chicken breasts, grilled, cut
        into strips
    1 cup seasoned croutons
  ½ cup KRAFT Shredded *or* 100% Grated Parmesan
        Cheese
  ¾ cup KRAFT FREE Caesar Italian Fat Free Dressing

TOSS lettuce, chicken, croutons and cheese in large salad bowl.

ADD dressing; toss to coat. Serve with fresh lemon wedges and fresh ground pepper, if desired.

Makes 4 servings

Variation: Prepare as directed, substituting 1 package (10 ounces) mixed or romaine salad greens.

Nutrition Information Per Serving: 240 calories, 7g total fat, 4g saturated fat, 55mg cholesterol, 1140mg sodium, 15g carbohydrate, 3g dietary fiber, 26g protein

Exchange: 2 Vegetable, ½ Carbohydrate, 3 Meat (L)

Grilled Chicken Caesar Salad

BBQ Ranch Chicken Salad

Prep: 15 minutes   **Cook:** 10 minutes

½ cup KRAFT Original Barbecue Sauce
 1 pound boneless skinless chicken breasts, cut into strips
 1 package (10 ounces) mixed salad greens
 1 large tomato, cut into wedges
½ cup sliced red onion
½ cup KRAFT LIGHT DONE RIGHT Ranch Reduced Fat
     Dressing
¼ cup crumbled blue cheese

HEAT barbecue sauce in skillet on medium-high heat. Add chicken; cook and stir until chicken is cooked through. Add additional barbecue sauce, if desired.

TOSS greens, tomato and onion in large bowl. Top with chicken. Pour dressing over greens mixture. Sprinkle with cheese.

Makes 6 servings

Variation: Place boneless skinless chicken breast halves on greased grill over medium coals. Grill 12 to 15 minutes or until cooked through, turning and brushing frequently with barbecue sauce. Slice chicken; serve over greens mixture.

Nutrition Information Per Serving: 170 calories, 7g total fat, 1.5g saturated fat, 55mg cholesterol, 370mg sodium, 6g carbohydrate, 2g dietary fiber, 20g protein

35% daily value vitamin A, 25% daily value vitamin C

Exchange: 2 Vegetable, 2 Meat (L)

Grilled Vegetable Kabob Salad

Prep: 15 minutes plus marinating   Grill: 8 minutes

1 *each* small green and red pepper, cut into 1-inch chunks
1 package (6 ounces) cremini *or* white mushrooms
1 small yellow summer squash, thickly sliced
1 small Vidalia *or* Walla Walla onion, cut into ¼-inch wedges
¾ cup KRAFT LIGHT DONE RIGHT Red Wine Vinegar Reduced Fat Dressing
8 cups torn assorted greens *or* 1 package (10 ounces) salad greens

ARRANGE vegetables alternately on 12 small skewers. Place in large pan; brush with dressing. Let stand 30 minutes to marinate.

PLACE skewers on grill over medium-hot coals.

GRILL 6 to 8 minutes or until vegetables are tender, brushing with dressing and turning occasionally. Place greens on 6 individual plates; top each with 2 kabobs.

Makes 6 servings

Nutrition Information Per Serving: 90 calories, 5g total fat, 0g saturated fat, 0mg cholesterol, 330mg sodium, 10g carbohydrate, 3g dietary fiber, 3g protein

45% daily value vitamin A, 60% daily value vitamin C

Exchange: 2 Vegetable, 1 Fat

Diabetic Choices

The Main Event

Your family will savor the flavor of these wonderful main dishes.

Barbecue Chicken Pizza

Prep: 15 minutes   Bake: 18 minutes

2 boneless skinless chicken breast halves
    (about ½ pound), cut into thin strips
1 green pepper, cut into strips
¼ cup thinly sliced red onion
1 prepared pizza crust (12 inch)
⅓ cup BULL'S-EYE *or* KRAFT Original Barbecue Sauce
1 cup KRAFT 2% Milk Shredded Reduced Fat
    Mozzarella Cheese
1 cup KRAFT FREE Fat Free Shredded Non-Fat
    Mozzarella Cheese

SPRAY large skillet with no stick cooking spray. Add chicken, green pepper and onion; cook on medium-high heat 4 to 5 minutes or until chicken is cooked through.

PLACE crust on cookie sheet. Spread with barbecue sauce. Top with chicken mixture and cheese.

BAKE at 400°F for 15 to 18 minutes or until cheese is melted and crust is golden brown.

Makes 4 servings

Continued on page 38

Diabetic Choices

On the Sidelines

Make your meals special with this exciting medley of salads and side dishes.

Italian Green Beans

Prep: 5 minutes   Cook: 10 minutes

½ cup water
1 package (16 ounces) frozen whole green beans
½ cup cubed POLLY-O Non-Fat Mozzarella Cheese (¼-inch cubes)
½ cup chopped seeded tomato
⅓ cup KRAFT FREE Italian Fat Free Dressing

BRING water to boil in medium saucepan. Add green beans; cook 2 minutes or until tender. Drain.

STIR in cheese, tomato and dressing. Serve hot.

Makes 6 servings

Nutrition Information Per Serving: 50 calories, 0g total fat, 0g saturated fat, 0mg cholesterol, 300mg sodium, 7g carbohydrate, 3g dietary fiber, 5g protein

10% daily value vitamin A, 15% daily value vitamin C

Exchange: 2 Vegetable

Roasted Potato and Vegetable Salad

Prep: 10 minutes   Bake: 45 minutes

2 pounds red potatoes, cubed
2 zucchini, thinly sliced lengthwise
2 carrots, diagonally sliced
1 small red onion, cut into wedges
2 cups KRAFT TASTE OF LIFE Tomato & Garlic Dressing

TOSS vegetables with dressing in large bowl.

SPOON into shallow roasting pan.

BAKE at 400°F for 40 to 45 minutes or until vegetables are tender, stirring occasionally.

Makes 8 servings

FIBER

Nutrition Information Per Serving: 230 calories, 10g total fat, 1g saturated fat, 0mg cholesterol, 500mg sodium, 32g carbohydrate, 4g dietary fiber, 4g protein

100% daily value vitamin A, 40% daily value vitamin C, 100% daily value vitamin E

Exchange: 1½ Starch, 1 Vegetable, 2 Fat

Roasted Potato and Vegetable Salad

Quick Italian Spinach Pie

Prep: 10 minutes   Bake: 40 minutes

1 container (16 ounces) BREAKSTONE'S *or* KNUDSEN
    2% Cottage Cheese
1 package (10 ounces) frozen chopped spinach,
    thawed, well drained
1 cup KRAFT Shredded Low-Moisture Part-Skim
    Mozzarella Cheese
4 eggs, beaten
1 jar (7 ounces) roasted red peppers, well drained,
    chopped
⅓ cup KRAFT 100% Grated Parmesan Cheese
1 teaspoon dried oregano leaves

MIX all ingredients.

POUR into greased 9-inch pie plate.

BAKE at 350°F for 40 minutes or until center is set.

Makes 8 servings

Variation: Prepare as directed, substituting ½ cup chopped red pepper for roasted red pepper.

CALCIUM

Nutrition Information Per Serving: 150 calories, 8g total fat, 4g saturated fat, 125mg cholesterol, 450mg sodium, 6g carbohydrate, 1g dietary fiber, 15g protein

50% daily value vitamin A, 25% daily value calcium

Exchange: 1 Vegetable, 2 Meat (L)

Quick Italian Spinach Pie

Diabetic Choices

Drinks on the House

This collection of thirst-quenching hot and cold beverages is sure to please young and old alike.

Fizzy Cran-Grape Lemonade Punch

Prep: 10 minutes

1 envelope KOOL-AID Sugar Free Lemonade Flavor Low
   Calorie Soft Drink Mix
1 bottle (48 ounces) chilled reduced-calorie cranberry-
   grape juice cocktail
1 bottle (1 liter) chilled seltzer
1 navel orange, sliced, cut into quarters
   Ice cubes *or* crushed ice

PLACE drink mix in large plastic or glass pitcher. Add cranberry-grape juice cocktail; stir to dissolve. Refrigerate.

POUR into large punch bowl just before serving. Stir in seltzer and oranges. Serve over ice.

Makes 2½ quarts or 10 (1-cup) servings

Nutrition Information Per Serving: 35 calories, 0g total fat, 0g saturated fat, 0mg cholesterol, 50mg sodium, 7g carbohydrate, 0g dietary fiber, less than 1g protein

90% daily value vitamin C

Exchange: ½ Fruit

Cool Yogurt Smoothie

Prep: 5 minutes

1 container (8 ounces) BREYERS Lowfat Yogurt, any
   flavor
2½ cups thawed COOL WHIP FREE Whipped Topping,
   divided
2 cups fresh or frozen strawberries *or any other*
   seasonal fruit, chopped
2 cups ice cubes

PLACE yogurt, 1½ cups of the whipped topping, fruit and
ice in blender container; cover. Blend until smooth. Top
each serving with ¼ cup of the remaining whipped topping.
Serve immediately.

Makes 4 (1-cup) servings

Breyers® is a registered trademark of Unilever, N.V., used under license.

FAT

Nutrition Information Per Serving: 110 calories, 2g total fat,
1.5g saturated fat, less than 5mg cholesterol, 40mg sodium,
23g carbohydrate, 2g dietary fiber, 3g protein

90% daily value vitamin C

Exchange: 1½ Carbohydrate

Top to bottom: Cool Yogurt Smoothie, Tropical Coffee Shake (page 73)

Diabetic Choices

Sweet Treats

Finally, here is an awesome array of dessert and snack recipes that are easy to prepare and fun to share.

Strawberry Short Cut

Prep: 10 minutes

1 package (13.6 ounces) fat-free pound cake
3 cups strawberries, sliced, sweetened
3¼ cups thawed COOL WHIP LITE Whipped Topping

CUT cake into 16 slices. Place 8 of the cake slices on individual dessert plates.

SPOON about 3 tablespoons of the strawberries over each cake slice. Top each with ¼ cup whipped topping. Repeat layers, ending with whipped topping. Serve immediately.

Makes 8 servings

Nutrition Information Per Serving: 270 calories, 2g total fat, 1.5g saturated fat, 0mg cholesterol, 170mg sodium, 64g carbohydrate, 3g dietary fiber, 3g protein

70% daily value vitamin C

Exchange: 4 Carbohydrate

Lemon Mousse with Raspberry Sauce

Prep: 5 minutes plus refrigerating

1½ cups boiling water
1 package (8-serving size) *or* 2 packages (4-serving size each) JELL-O Brand Lemon Flavor Sugar Free Low Calorie Gelatin
2 teaspoons grated lemon peel
1 cup cold apple juice
Ice cubes
1 tub (8 ounces) COOL WHIP FREE Whipped Topping, thawed
1 package (10 ounces) frozen raspberries *or* strawberries, thawed, puréed in blender

STIR boiling water into gelatin and lemon peel in large bowl at least 2 minutes until gelatin is completely dissolved. Mix apple juice and ice to measure 1¾ cups. Add to gelatin, stirring until slightly thickened. Remove any remaining ice.

STIR in whipped topping with wire whisk. Pour into serving bowl or 10 dessert dishes.

REFRIGERATE 4 hours or until firm. Serve with raspberry sauce.

Makes 10 servings

Nutrition Information Per Serving: 80 calories, 1.5g total fat, 1g saturated fat, 0mg cholesterol, 60mg sodium, 15g carbohydrate, 2g dietary fiber, 2g protein

10% daily value vitamin C

Exchange: 1 Carbohydrate

Bran Fruit and Nut Cookies

Prep: 15 minutes   **Bake:** 10 minutes

½ cup firmly packed brown sugar
¼ cup oil
2 tablespoons water
2 egg whites, slightly beaten
1 teaspoon ground cinnamon
½ teaspoon baking soda
⅛ teaspoon salt
1 cup flour
1 ½ cups POST Raisin Bran Cereal
¼ cup chopped walnuts
¼ cup chopped dried apricots (optional)

MIX sugar, oil, water, egg whites, cinnamon, baking soda and salt in large bowl. Stir in flour and cereal. Mix in walnuts and apricots.

DROP by rounded teaspoons onto lightly greased cookie sheets.

BAKE at 350°F for 10 minutes or until browned. Remove and cool on wire racks. Store in tightly covered container.

Makes 4 dozen

Nutrition Information Per Serving (3 cookies): 130 calories, 5g total fat, 0.5g saturated fat, 0mg cholesterol, 115mg sodium, 20g carbohydrate, 1g dietary fiber, 2g protein

Exchange: 1 Carbohydrate, 1 Fat

Banana Cinnamon Spice Pie

Prep: 10 minutes plus refrigerating

1 large ripe banana, sliced
1 prepared reduced-fat graham cracker crumb crust
    (6 ounce *or* 9 inch)
1½ cups cold fat-free milk
2 packages (4-serving size each) JELL-O White
    Chocolate *or* Vanilla Flavor Fat Free Sugar Free
    Instant Reduced Calorie Pudding & Pie Filling
½ teaspoon ground cinnamon
1 tub (8 ounces) COOL WHIP FREE Whipped Topping,
    thawed

PLACE banana slices in bottom of crust.

POUR milk into large bowl. Add pudding mixes and cinnamon. Beat with wire whisk 1 minute. Gently stir in whipped topping. Spoon into crust. Sprinkle with additional cinnamon, if desired.

REFRIGERATE 4 hours or until set.

Makes 8 servings

Nutrition Information Per Serving: 210 calories, 5g total fat, 2.5g saturated fat, 0mg cholesterol, 460mg sodium, 38g carbohydrate, 1g dietary fiber, 3g protein

Exchange: 2½ Carbohydrate, ½ Fat

Banana Cinnamon Spice Pie

Tiramisu

Prep: 15 minutes plus refrigerating

⅓ cup GENERAL FOODS INTERNATIONAL COFFEES,
　　Sugar Free Fat Free Suisse Mocha Flavor, divided
2 tablespoons hot water
1 package (3 ounces) ladyfingers, split
2½ cups cold fat-free milk, divided
1 container (8 ounces) PHILADELPHIA FREE Soft Fat Free
　　Cream Cheese
2 packages (4-serving size each) JELL-O Vanilla Flavor
　　Fat Free Sugar Free Instant Reduced Calorie
　　Pudding & Pie Filling
1 cup thawed COOL WHIP LITE Whipped Topping

DISSOLVE 1 tablespoon of the flavored instant coffee in hot water in small bowl.

COVER bottom and sides of shallow 2-quart dessert dish with ladyfingers. Sprinkle dissolved flavored instant coffee over ladyfingers.

PLACE ½ cup of the milk, cream cheese and remaining undissolved flavored instant coffee in blender container; cover. Blend on medium speed until smooth. Add pudding mixes and remaining 2 cups milk; cover. Blend on medium speed until smooth. Carefully pour into prepared bowl. Top with whipped topping.

REFRIGERATE at least 3 hours or until set. Just before serving, sprinkle with additional undissolved flavored instant coffee, if desired.

Makes 12 servings

Nutrition Information Per Serving:　100 calories, 2g total fat, 1g saturated fat, 30mg cholesterol, 370mg sodium, 16g carbohydrate, 0g dietary fiber, 6g protein

10% daily value vitamin A, 10% daily value calcium

Exchange:　1 Carbohydrate, ½ Fat

Tiramisu

Mocha Pudding Parfaits

Prep: 10 minutes plus refrigerating

1½ cups cold fat-free milk
   1 tablespoon MAXWELL HOUSE Instant Coffee
   1 package (4-serving size) JELL-O Chocolate Flavor Fat
      Free Sugar Free Instant Reduced Calorie Pudding
      & Pie Filling
   1 tub (8 ounces) COOL WHIP FREE Whipped Topping,
      thawed, divided
   6 reduced-fat chocolate wafer cookies, chopped

POUR milk and instant coffee into medium bowl. Add pudding mix. Beat with wire whisk 1 minute. Gently stir in ½ of the whipped topping.

SPOON ½ of the pudding mixture evenly into 6 dessert dishes. Sprinkle with chopped cookies.

COVER with ½ of the remaining whipped topping. Top with remaining pudding mixture. Garnish each serving with a spoonful of remaining whipped topping.

REFRIGERATE until ready to serve.

Makes 6 servings

FAT

Nutrition Information Per Serving: 130 calories, 2.5g total fat, 2g saturated fat, 0mg cholesterol, 280mg sodium, 26g carbohydrate, less than 1g dietary fiber, 3g protein

Exchange: 1½ Carbohydrate, ½ Fat

Mocha Pudding Parfaits

Low Fat Watergate Salad

Prep: 10 minutes plus refrigerating

1 package (4-serving size) JELL-O Pistachio Flavor Fat
    Free Sugar Free Instant Reduced Calorie Pudding
    & Pie Filling
1 can (8 ounces) crushed pineapple in juice, undrained
1 container (8 ounces) BREYERS Vanilla Lowfat Yogurt
2 cups plus 6 tablespoons thawed COOL WHIP FREE
    Whipped Topping, divided

STIR pudding mix, pineapple with juice and yogurt in large
bowl until well blended. Gently stir in 2 cups of the
whipped topping.

REFRIGERATE 1 hour or until ready to serve. Top each
serving with 1 tablespoon remaining whipped topping.

Makes 6 servings

Breyers® is a registered trademark of Unilever, N. V., used under license.

Nutrition Information Per Serving: 130 calories, 2g total fat,
2g saturated fat, less than 5mg cholesterol, 220mg sodium,
26g carbohydrate, 0g dietary fiber, 2g protein

Exchange: 1½ Carbohydrate

Index

Ice Cream
COUNTRY TIME® Lemon Creamy Frosty, 72
Tropical Coffee Shake, 73

Italian Green Beans, 54
Italian Vegetable Salad, 63

JELL-O® 'n Juice Parfaits, 86
JELL-O® Juicy JIGGLERS®, 85

KRAFT® TASTE OF LIFE™ Salad, 59

Lemon Mousse with Raspberry Sauce, 80
Low Fat Watergate Salad, 92

Mediterranean Wrap Sandwich, 14
Mocha Pudding Parfaits, 90

Mushrooms
Bacon and Creamy Fettuccine, 40
Broccoli & Carrot Salad, 58
Easy Italian Vegetable Pasta Bake, 47
Grilled Vegetable Kabob Salad, 35
20 Minute Chicken & Brown Rice Pilaf, 48
Zesty Shrimp and Pasta, 50

My Hero, 10

Oranges
Fizzy Cran-Grape Lemonade Punch, 66
Spinach & Orange Salad, 60

Pasta
Bacon and Creamy Fettuccine, 40
Bistro Chicken Pasta Salad, 28
Creamy Bow Tie Primavera, 52
DI GIORNO® Easy Chicken Cacciatore with Light Ravioli, 38
Easy Italian Vegetable Pasta Bake, 47
Italian Vegetable Salad, 63
Stuffed Shells, 53
Zesty Shrimp and Pasta, 50

Pear & Raspberry Salad, 62

Pies
Banana Cinnamon Spice Pie, 82
Quick Italian Spinach Pie, 64

Potatoes: Roasted Potato and Vegetable Salad, 56

Quick Italian Spinach Pie, 64

Rice
Crab and Rice Primavera, 46
Simply Sensational Stir-Fry, 39
20 Minute Chicken & Brown Rice Pilaf, 48
Roasted Potato and Vegetable Salad, 56

Salsa Turkey Grill, 17

Shrimp
Spicy Asian Shrimp Salad, 26
Zesty Shrimp and Pasta, 50

Simply Sensational Stir-Fry, 39
Spicy Asian Shrimp Salad, 26

Spinach
KRAFT® TASTE OF LIFE™ Salad, 59
Quick Italian Spinach Pie, 64
Spinach & Orange Salad, 60
Stuffed Shells, 53

Spinach & Orange Salad, 60
Strawberry Short Cut, 78
Stuffed Shells, 53
Sunny Orange Delight, 72
Sunrise Punch, 74

Tangy Grilled Chicken Kabobs, 44
Tiramisu, 88

Tomatoes, Fresh
Bacon and Creamy Fettuccine, 40
BBQ Ranch Chicken Salad, 34
Bistro Chicken Pasta Salad, 28
Creamy Cucumber Salad, 62
Creamy Ranch & Parmesan Chicken Salad, 24
Greek Chicken Salad, 25
Grilled Steak Salad, 22
KRAFT® TASTE OF LIFE™ Salad, 59
My Hero, 10
Vegetable Turkey Pockets, 8

Tropical Coffee Shake, 73

Turkey
Club Calzone, 18
Mediterranean Wrap Sandwich, 14
My Hero, 10
Salsa Turkey Grill, 17
Vegetable Turkey Pockets, 8
20 Minute Chicken & Brown Rice Pilaf, 48

Vegetable Pita Pockets, 13
Vegetable Turkey Pockets, 8

White Chocolate Orange Mousse, 84

Zesty Shrimp and Pasta, 50

Zucchini
Easy Italian Vegetable Pasta Bake, 47
Italian Vegetable Salad, 63
Roasted Potato and Vegetable Salad, 56

METRIC CONVERSION CHART

VOLUME MEASUREMENTS (dry)

1/8 teaspoon = 0.5 mL
1/4 teaspoon = 1 mL
1/2 teaspoon = 2 mL
3/4 teaspoon = 4 mL
1 teaspoon = 5 mL
1 tablespoon = 15 mL
2 tablespoons = 30 mL
1/4 cup = 60 mL
1/3 cup = 75 mL
1/2 cup = 125 mL
2/3 cup = 150 mL
3/4 cup = 175 mL
1 cup = 250 mL
2 cups = 1 pint = 500 mL
3 cups = 750 mL
4 cups = 1 quart = 1 L

VOLUME MEASUREMENTS (fluid)

1 fluid ounce (2 tablespoons) = 30 mL
4 fluid ounces (1/2 cup) = 125 mL
8 fluid ounces (1 cup) = 250 mL
12 fluid ounces (1 1/2 cups) = 375 mL
16 fluid ounces (2 cups) = 500 mL

WEIGHTS (mass)

1/2 ounce = 15 g
1 ounce = 30 g
3 ounces = 90 g
4 ounces = 120 g
8 ounces = 225 g
10 ounces = 285 g
12 ounces = 360 g
16 ounces = 1 pound = 450 g

DIMENSIONS

1/16 inch = 2 mm
1/8 inch = 3 mm
1/4 inch = 6 mm
1/2 inch = 1.5 cm
3/4 inch = 2 cm
1 inch = 2.5 cm

OVEN TEMPERATURES

250°F = 120°C
275°F = 140°C
300°F = 150°C
325°F = 160°C
350°F = 180°C
375°F = 190°C
400°F = 200°C
425°F = 220°C
450°F = 230°C

BAKING PAN SIZES

Utensil	Size in Inches/Quarts	Metric Volume	Size in Centimeters
Baking or Cake Pan (square or rectangular)	8×8×2	2 L	20×20×5
	9×9×2	2.5 L	23×23×5
	12×8×2	3 L	30×20×5
	13×9×2	3.5 L	33×23×5
Loaf Pan	8×4×3	1.5 L	20×10×7
	9×5×3	2 L	23×13×7
Round Layer Cake Pan	8×1½	1.2 L	20×4
	9×1½	1.5 L	23×4
Pie Plate	8×1¼	750 mL	20×3
	9×1¼	1 L	23×
Baking Dish or Casserole	1 quart	1 L	
	1½ quart	1.5 L	
	2 quart	2 L